D1382668

◄ T H E ►
CANADIANS

Biographies of a Nation

Omnibus Edition

Patrick Watson

McArthur & Company
Toronto

First published by McArthur & Company in 2003
McArthur & Company,
322 King Street West, Suite 402, Toronto, ON, M5V 1J2
www.mcarthur-co.com

National Library of Canada Cataloguing in Publication

Watson, Patrick, 1929-
    The Canadians : biographies of a nation omnibus / Patrick Watson.

    Original 3rd vol. written by Patrick Watson and Hugh Graham.
    Companion volume to the television series,
    Canadians: biographies of a nation.
    Includes bibliographical references.
    ISBN 1-55278-390-1

    1. Canada—Biography. 2. Canadians : biographies of a nation
    (Television program). I. Graham, Hugh, 1951- II. Title.

    FC25.W37 2003   971'.009'9   C2003-904449-1

Composition/Cover/Photo f/x: *Mad Dog Design Inc.*
Printed in Canada by *Friesens*

Credits for cover photographs:
Fred Rose: Canadian Tribune/*National Archives of Canada/PA-126570*
Samuel Cunard: *National Archives of Canada/PA-124022/Courtesy of Tri Media Productions*
John Ware: *Glenbow Archives/NA-263-1*
Pauline Johnson w/Feather Boa/*Courtesy of the Brant County Museum & Archives*
Ruth Lowe: *Tom Sandler*
Sam Hughes: *Courtesy of The National Archives of Canada/PA-121719*
Northrop Frye: *Courtesy of Tom Sandler*
Wop May: *Courtesy of Denny May*

The publisher would like to acknowledge the financial support of the Government
of Canada through the Book Publishing Industry Development Program, the
Canada Council, and the Ontario Arts Council for our publishing activities.
We also acknowledge the Government of Ontario through the Ontario Media
Development Corporation Ontario Book Initiative.

10 9 8 7 6 5 4 3 2 1